Christmas, 1980

Dear Joan:

Thank you for your "being" in my life; you are the channel of so much that is precious to me today.

Love,
Marty

GEOGRAPHY OF HOLINESS

GEOGRAPHY OF HOLINESS

THE PHOTOGRAPHY OF
THOMAS MERTON

Edited by Deba Prasad Patnaik   The Pilgrim Press · New York

Library of Congress Cataloging in Publication Data

Merton, Thomas, 1915–1968.
  Geography of holiness.

  Includes bibliographical references.
  1. Photography, Artistic. 2. Merton, Thomas, 1915–
1968. I. Patnaik, Deba Prasad. II. Title.
TR654.M4633 1980   779'.092'4   80–18604
ISBN 0–8298–0401–3

The publisher wishes to express appreciation for permission to reprint copyrighted material.

Excerpt from LOVE AND LIVING by Thomas Merton. Copyright © 1965, 1966, 1967, 1968, 1969, 1977, 1979 by The Trustees of the Merton Legacy Trust. Reprinted by permission of Farrar, Straus & Giroux, Inc.

Excerpts from THE SIGN OF JONAS by Thomas Merton are reprinted by permission of Harcourt Brace Jovanovich, Inc.; copyright © 1953 by The Abbey of Our Lady of Gethsemani.

Excerpts from the following are reprinted by permission of New Directions Publishing Corporation: RAIDS ON THE UNSPEAKABLE by Thomas Merton, copyright © 1966 by The Abbey of Gethsemani, Inc.; NEW SEEDS OF CONTEMPLATION by Thomas Merton, copyright © 1961 by The Abbey of Gethsemani, Inc.; THE ASIAN JOURNAL by Thomas Merton, copyright © 1973 by The Trustees of the Merton Legacy Trust; COLLECTED POEMS by Thomas Merton, copyright © 1957, 1963 by The Abbey of Gethsemani, Inc., copyright © 1969 by The Trustees of the Merton Legacy Trust.

Copyright © 1980 The Pilgrim Press
All rights reserved

No part of this publication may be reproduced, stored in a retrieval system, or transmitted in any form or by any means, electronic, mechanical, photocopying, recording, or otherwise (brief quotations used in magazines or newspaper reviews excepted), without the prior permission of the publisher.

The Pilgrim Press, 132 W. 31 Street, New York, New York 10001

for John Howard Griffin, an unusual friend

for Karunya, my son

Acknowledgments

I thank Naomi Burton Stone, James Laughlin, and Tommie O'Callaghan, members of the Thomas Merton Legacy Trust, for their cooperation and permission to use Merton's photographs and texts in the book. Dr. Robert E. Daggy, Curator of the Merton Center in Louisville, has given me his best services.

Mrs. Anne H. McCormick, Administrator of the Legacy, has been exceptionally helpful and encouraging. I am much beholden to her.

My friends Patsy Horan, Gabrielle Beard, Virginia Baron, and Charlie Traub, Director of the Light Gallery in New York, have extended crucial support; Sue and Leon Driskell have generously given me various kinds of assistance and advice.

Christina Clarke and Linn Underhill deserve my gratitude and appreciation for all their expert technical help and suggestions.

I am most grateful to Brother Patrick Hart of the Abbey of Gethsemani for his friendship, guidance, and prayers.

I am fortunate to have Esther Cohen as my editor. Her enthusiasm and kindness have been of utmost value. Her colleagues at The Pilgrim Press, Paul Sherry and Joe Stuart, have been very supportive.

Karunya and Annya, my wife, have sustained me with their inspiration, joy and help.

My initial feeling has now become a conviction—the fulfillment of this work is an act of Divine magic. And, that extraordinary contemplative, Father Louis, has singularly informed my endeavours.

Foreword

This book is a selection of one hundred photographs taken by Thomas Merton during his brief but serious involvement with photography. This first published collection focuses on Merton's distinct photographic artistry. In Kentucky, New Mexico, California, Alaska, India, Sri Lanka, or Thailand, Merton used the camera with remarkable directness, precision, and sensitivity. Anything was material for Merton: a wooden stool, wheel, basket, rocks, roots, woods, trees, snow, paint buckets, chairs, boats, rivers, oceans, statues, structures, and faces. His acute eye and poetic sensibility caught the magic play of light on natural and man-made objects in striking abstract and surrealistic forms. His imagery evokes profound aesthetic perception as well as a rare sense of the holiness of all created things. Centered in his religious vocation as a Trappist, Merton, through his artistic gifts, has created a visual world of joy, strength, and inspiration.

Quotes from Thomas Merton's journals, philosophical and religious prose, and poetry accompany the photographs to recreate the ambiance of his life and the specific moods and feelings of his images. His texts heighten our enjoyment and appreciation of his photography. In his Introduction and Afterword, poet, photographer, critic Deba P. Patnaik, who knew Merton well, draws from Merton's own writings and from those of eminent modern photographers such as Alfred Stieglitz, Edward Weston, and Ansel Adams to show the integration of Merton's aesthetic notions and his own art.

Introduction

This day will not come again; the air full of courtesies; birds fly uncorrected; trees click in the wind like rosaries; the sun rides like a piker through flowering trees. He walks past a long avenue of trees—sweet gums, sycamores, elms, gingkos. A mechanical device hangs from the neck of his dark blue work-shirt to the weathered leather belt and baggy denim pants. He is of average height; with stubby fingers, strong working hands, bald head, but, his eyes—*waterfalls of silence.* He winds down narrow, dirt roads, over green, rolling hills. Today, he feels, *the land is alive with miracles.* He senses *a new presence in the sun. Brilliant syllable of such an intuition, turns within . . . plunges after to discover flame.* He lifts the box to his eyes, clicks it to seize the moment—a huge, dried root whose fingers rhythm upward, trees that are *dens of light and boom with honey bees, orchards dream in the noon.* His eyes sparkle; he smiles. *There is no evil in anything created by God . . . everything made by God is good,* he murmurs to himself; drops the camera to his waist. It does not belong to him. He owns nothing, for poverty, voluntary poverty, is his vow. A trusted friend lent it to him, and, with the curiousity and wonderment of a child, he plays with the camera. He uses it as a means of great enjoyment, another way toward the condition of prayer. The outcome of this approach illuminates the quality of his feeling, his vision.

Seeing for Thomas Merton is a singular faculty and function. "We must," he writes in *The Monastic Journey*, "begin by learning *how to use and respect* the visible creation which mirrors the glory of the invisible God."[1] In *Conjectures of a Guilty Bystander,* he emphasizes the need "to *see* directly what is right in front of us."[2] The nature of Merton's "seeing" is "to look into the essences of things," to quote Herakleitos, whose ideas he assimilated in his writings. Cave art he says is, "a sign of pure seeing, nothing else."[3] Merton, though not erudite in photography literature, comes instinctively close to Edward Weston's ideas of "seeing more than the eye sees," and to see "the quintessence of the thing itself."[4] Two passages in *The Asian Journal* further elucidate Merton's view. On November 19, 1968, he observes:

> I took three more photos of the mountain (the *Kanchenjunga* in the Himalayas). An act of reconciliation? No, a camera cannot reconcile one with anything. Nor can it see a real mountain. The camera does not know what it takes: it captures materials with which you reconstruct, not so much what you saw as what you thought you saw. Hence the best photography is aware, mindful, of illusion and uses illusion, permitting and encouraging it—especially unconscious and powerful illusions that are not normally admitted in the scene.[5]

This curious passage needs to be read along with what he writes a little later:

> The full beauty of the mountain is not seen until you consent to the impossible paradox: it is and is not. When nothing more needs to be said, the smoke of ideas clears, the mountain is SEEN.[6]

These passages constitute a subtle and succinct statement about the magic involved in the creative process of making a picture: the very ideas and concepts maintained by masters of modern photography.

The realm of art, of photography, Merton holds, is "the realm of intuition."[7] The artist is both a "maker" and a "seer."[8] The artist is not one who is just reproducing things, but "creating something new, an *ikon,* an image which embodies the inner truth of things as they exist in the world of intelligible being."[9] Merton suggests that the transformation of object to image clarifies and reveals meanings, which, in turn, also transcend the meaning of the object as thing in itself. This attitude in no way contradicts his "unspeakable reverence for the holiness of created things."[10] One notices how his photographs allow the objects their own autonomy and fidelity, and yet reflect a "reality which is perceived spiritually in the artist's own soul."[11] Images of roots, trees, a basket filled with light and shadow, an off-centered fence with sticks and wires, or images of bricks, two tumblers, and a cup and saucer on a table exemplify Merton's aesthetic—a process of understanding the essence of objects. This multifaction of objects, images, and meanings has a mystery of its own grounded in Merton's act of being as a contemplative and an artist.

The personality of Thomas Merton (Father Louis of the Abbey of Gethsemani) was multi-dimensional; his interests and involvements, his tastes and attitudes, genuine and varied. Far from being a "conventional" monk, he defied categories. His gregarious and eclectic character troubled some, who often questioned his vocation. Merton responds humorously and tellingly:

> The contemplative life is unfortunately too often thought of in terms purely of "enclosure," and monks are conceived of as hothouse plants, nursed along in a carefully protected and spiritually overheated life of prayer. But let us remember that the contemplative life is first of all *life,* and life implies openness, growth, development.[12]

In *The Sign of Jonas*, he talks about his own life "alone and chaste in the midst of the holy beauty of all created things," which are "mirrors of His beauty."[13] "My being," he continues in *Conjectures of a Guilty Bystander,* "is given me . . . as a source of joy, growth, life, creativity, and fulfillment."[14] He finds it perverse to regard spontaneity and enjoyment as "a sinful gratification of 'fallen nature.'"[15] Rejecting the dichotomy of sense and spirit, he affirms in "Notes on Art and Worship":

> The world of the spirit is not something quite apart from the world of the senses. The two are in fact inseparable and form a single whole. Man, the image of God, has a vocation not only to rule and cultivate the world, but to transform it and draw forth from it the spiritual glory which has been hidden in it by the Creator.[16]

This fundamental conviction informs Merton's work and finds expression in his writings. The extract from "Notes" underlines his cardinal beliefs—cosmic connectedness, wholeness, and incarnational dynamics. *Hagia Sophia* declares:

> There is in all visible things an invisible fecundity, a dimmed light, a meek namelessness, a hidden wholeness. This mysterious Unity and Integrity is Wisdom, the Mother of all, *Natura Naturans.*
> There is in all things an inexhaustible sweetness

and purity, a silence that is a fountain of action and joy.[17]

Merton's life, both as eremite and artist, derives validity and strength from these beliefs. He finds no contradiction or opposition in the life which fuses both the modes. He maintains:

> In actual fact, neither religious nor artistic contemplation should be regarded as "things" which happen or "objects" which one can "have." They belong to the much more mysterious realm of what one "is"—rather "who" one is. Aesthetic intuition is not merely the act of a faculty, it is also a heightening and intensification of our personal identity and being by the perception of our connatural affinity with "Being" in the beauty contemplated.[18]

In the words of Stieglitz, "All art is but a picture of certain basic relationships: an *equivalent* of the artist's most profound experience of life."[19]

For Merton, matters of personal identity, the quality and nature of life-experience, and of his relationship with the universe around, assume a unique importance. He had found writing "one of the conditions on which my perfection will depend . . . with most complete simplicity and integrity."[20] So, too, with his visual arts, specifically photography. The "special inspiration" Jacques Maritain talks about, or Rouault's "interior light," operates in Merton's photographic expression: communion. As he suggests in his thoughtful essay, "Theology of Creativity," true creativity produces a "free and spontaneous person" moving toward self-realization, confronting life through artistic integrity and creative communication.[21] In "Notes on Art and Worship," he explains:

> By artistic and creative genius, man rises above the material elements and outer appearances of things and sees into their inner nature.[22]

Further, "Man cannot be fully himself if he is only a scientist and a technician: he must also be an artist and contemplative."[23] Here again Merton equates the artist and the contemplative together. "Art," he asserts in *The Sign of Jonas,* "demands asceticism."[24] Exactly as his "typewriter is an essential factor in [his] asceticism,"[25] his use of the camera becomes integral to his contemplative life.

Deba P. Patnaik

GEOGRAPHY OF HOLINESS

For the world and time are the dance of the Lord in emptiness. The silence of the spheres is the music of a wedding feast. The more we persist in misunderstanding the phenomena of life, the more we analyze them out into strange finalities and complex purposes of our own, the more we involve ourselves in sadness, absurdity and despair. But it does not matter much, because no despair of ours can alter the reality of things, or stain the joy of the cosmic dance which is always there.[1]

I am able to approach the Buddhas barefoot and undisturbed, my feet in wet grass, wet sand. Then the silence of the extraordinary faces. The great smiles. Huge and yet subtle. Filled with every possibility, questioning nothing, knowing everything, rejecting nothing, the peace not of emotional resignation but of Madhyamika, of sunyata, that has seen through every question without trying to discredit anyone or anything—*without refutation*—without establishing some other argument. For the doctrinaire, the mind that needs well-established positions, such peace, such silence, can be frightening. I was knocked over with a rush of relief and thankfulness at the *obvious* clarity and fluidity of shape and line, the design of the monumental bodies composed into the rock shape and landscape, figure, rock and tree. And the sweep of bare rock sloping away on the other side of the hollow, where you can go back and see different aspects of the figures.

Looking at these figures I was suddenly, almost forcibly, jerked clean out of the habitual, half-tied vision of things, and an inner clearness, clarity, as if exploding from the rocks themselves, became evident and obvious. The queer *evidence* of the reclining figure, the smile, the sad smile of Ananda standing with arms folded (much more "imperative" than Da Vinci's Mona Lisa because completely simple and straightforward). The thing about all this is that there is no puzzle, no problem, and really no "mystery." All problems are resolved and everything is clear, simply because what matters is clear. The rock, all matter, all life, is charged with dharmakaya . . . everything is emptiness and everything is compassion.[2]

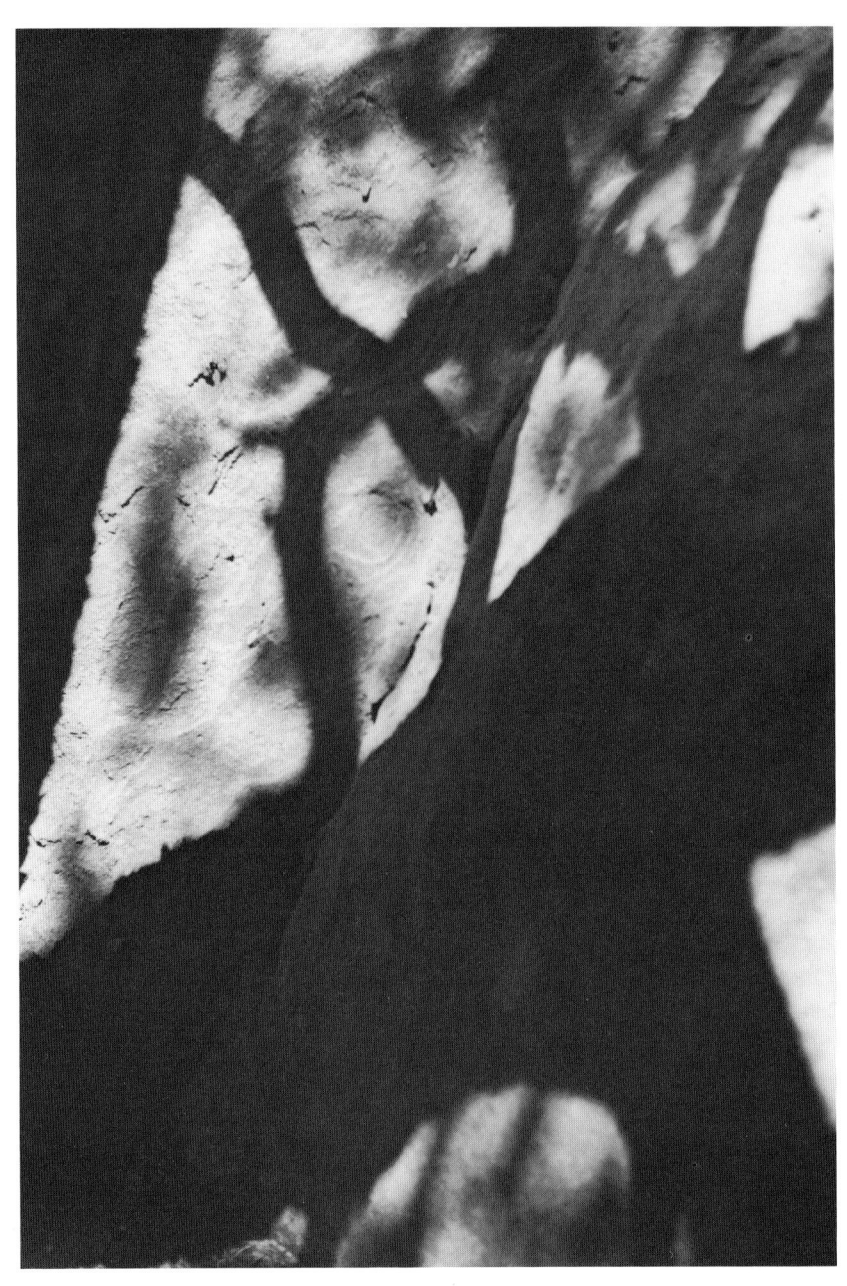

To have passed there
Walked without a word
To have felt
All my old grounds
Forgotten world
All along
Dream places
Words in my feet
Explain the air of all
Feel under (me)
Stand
Stand in the unspoken
A cool street
An air of legs
An air of vision.

Geography
I am all (here)
There![3]

There is no water in the shales that was not hidden there by Your wisdom. . . .

But there is greater comfort in the substance of silence than in the answer to a question. Eternity is in the present. Eternity is in the palm of the hand. Eternity is a seed of fire, whose sudden roots break barriers that keep my heart from being an abyss.

The things of Time are in connivance with eternity. The shadows serve You. . . . The solid hills shall vanish like a worn out garment. All things change, and die and disappear. Questions arrive, assume their actuality, and also disappear. In this hour I shall cease to ask them, and silence shall be my answer.[4]

A yellow flower
(Light and spirit)
Sings by itself
For nobody.

A golden spirit
(Light and emptiness)
Sings without a word
By itself.

Let no one touch this gentle sun
In whose dark eye
Someone is awake.

(No light, no gold, no name, no color
And no thought:
O, wide awake!)

A golden heaven
Sings by itself
A song to nobody.[5]

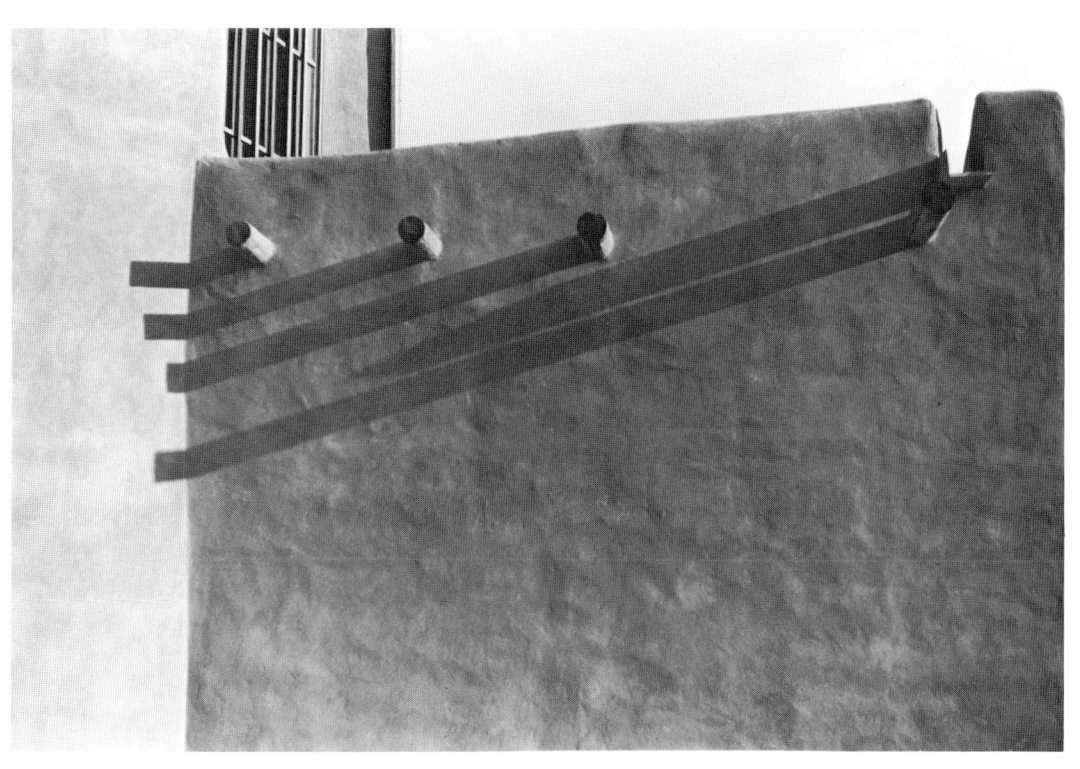

The three doors (they are one door.)

1) The door of emptiness. Of no-where. Of no place for a self, which cannot be entered by a self. . . . Is it a door at all? The door of no-door.

2) The door without sign, without indicator, without information. . . . But do not look for a sign saying "Not-Door." Or even "No Exit."

3) The door without wish. The undesired. The unplanned door. . . . Door without aim. Door without end. Does not respond to a key—so do not imagine you have a key.

There is no use asking for it. Yet you must ask. Who? For what? . . . Do not be deceived into thinking this door is merely hard to find and difficult to open. When sought it fades. Recedes. Diminishes. Is nothing. There is no threshold. . . . It is not empty space. . . . Because it has no foundation, it is the end of sorrow. . . . Such is the door that ends all doors; the unbuilt, the impossible, the undestroyed, through which all the fires go when they have "gone out."[7]

We *are* the world. . . . Through our senses and our minds, our loves, needs, and desires, we are implicated, without possibility of evasion, in this world of matters and of men, of things and of persons, which not only affect us and change our lives but are also affected and changed by us. From the moment we sit down at the table and put a piece of bread in our mouths, we see that we are in the world and cannot be otherwise than in it, until the day we die. The question, then, is not to speculate about how we are to contact the world—as if we were somehow in outer space—but how to validate our relationship, give it a fully honest and human significance, and make it truly productive and worthwhile for our world.[8]

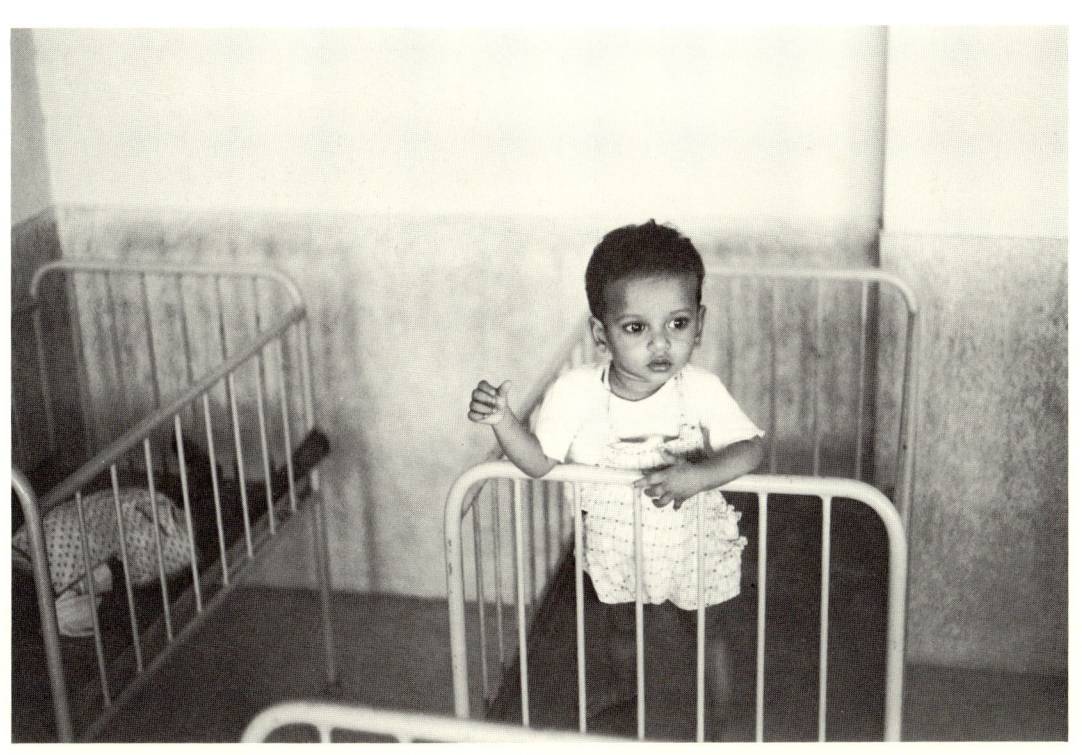

The free man is not alone as busy men are
But as birds are. The free man sings
Alone as universes do. Built
Upon his own inscrutable pattern
Clear, unmistakable, not invented by himself alone
Or for himself, but for the universe also.[9]

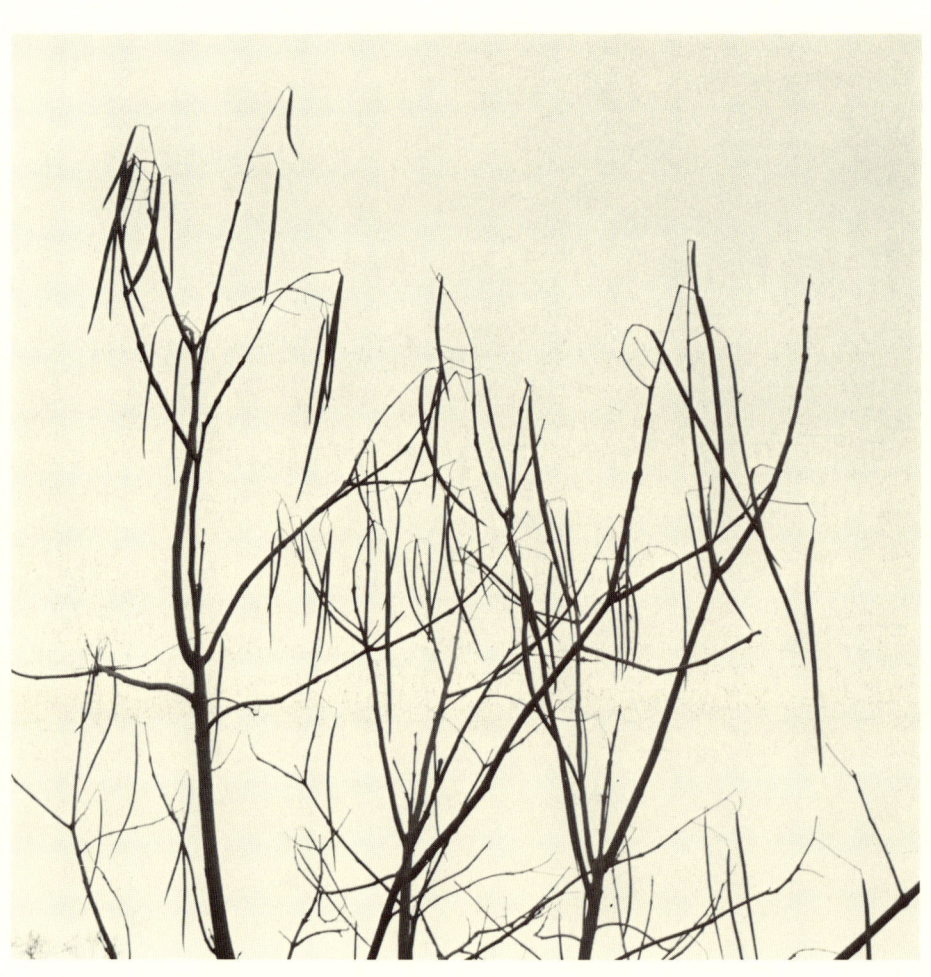

But there is a higher light still, not the light by which man "gives names" and forms concepts, with the aid of the active intelligence, but the dark light in which no names are given, in which God confronts man not through medium of things, but in His own simplicity. The union of the simple light of God with the simple light of man's spirit, in love, is contemplation.[10]

There is a justice of newborn worlds which cannot be counted. There is a mercy of individual things that spring into being without reason. . . . Every plant that stands in the light of the sun is a saint and an outlaw. Every tree that brings forth blossoms without the command of man is powerful in the sight of God. Every star that man has not counted is a world of sanity and perfection. Every blade of grass is an angel singing in a shower of glory.

These are worlds of themselves. No man can use or destroy them. There is life that moves without being seen and cannot be understood. . . . The fire of a wild white sun has eaten up the distance between hope and despair. Dance in this sun you tepid idiot. Wake up and dance in the clarity of perfect contradiction.[11]

In my ending is my meaning.[12]

Afterword

Thomas Merton was not a "professional" photographer; photography was not his lifelong passion or primary involvement in life. Except for Eugene Meatyard, Shirley Burden, and John Howard Griffin, he did not have photographer friends. Nor does one find photography books in his library. But, photography "fascinates me," he wrote to Griffin in 1963; he was impressed by the wisdom of Griffin's lenses.[1] He admired Meatyard's imagery, so unlike his own. He took, it seems, very few pictures during the early 60s.

His serious engagement with photography began in 1966, when Griffin gave him on a permanent loan a Canon F-X. At first, Griffin notes, Merton often asked, "What am I doing wrong?"[2] Griffin tells me his comments and advice to Merton were minimal because the photographs already showed remarkable competence and dedication. From the negatives left behind (a surprisingly large collection), we know he used three different kinds of cameras—a Rollieflex, a Kodak instamatic, and a Canon F-X. But, whenever Griffin visited him at the Gethsemani Monastery, he used Griffin's Alpa, which Merton labelled the "Picasso Camera," since Douglas Duncan used a similar one for his books on the painter. Of the one hundred photographs in this book, only Maritain's portrait was taken with the Alpa, while numbers 12, 19, 23, 33, 66, 67, 72, 76, and 84 were taken with a Rollieflex, and 6, 14, 18, 34, 55, 61, 65, and 77 with an instamatic, and the rest with a Canon F-X. Distressingly, Merton did not live long enough to see the superb photographs he took during his trip to New Mexico, California, Alaska, and Asia in late 1968.

Merton could not process and print his films in the Monastery, for such facilities were not available to him. Griffin regularly supplied him with film; he and his son, Greg, processed and printed the film rolls. On contact sheets, Merton would mark his instructions and send them to Griffin for the final prints. In examining these sheets and his letters to both the father and son, I find few special darkroom directions, only instruction to crop a few negatives. He did not care for darkroom tricks and manipulations, nor did he stage photographs. He framed and shot with forthrightness, sensitively capturing images at precise creative moments. This indicates his integrity of approach and execution. Most of the time, he shot but once, although there are several shots of the same object until he was able to capture his vision accurately and completely. Numbers 2, 6, 10, 14, 37, 56, 71, 73, 89, 97, and 98 are some examples of his single shots. Rocks, roots, and trees intrigued him, symbolically and materially; he took numerous pictures of them. Roots, trees, chairs, paint buckets, rocks, landscapes, structures, and faces express Merton's sensibility in conveying life with simplicity and understanding, wit and subtlety. If one finds wit and humor in some (e.g. 25 and 83), there is simplicity and evocativeness in others (6, 7, 21, 30, 51, 52, 99); surprise and subtlety in some others (34, 39, 56, 71, 73). The sense of relationship, sharpness of design and composition, and metaphoric abstraction in images, such as 1, 8, 11, 16, 17, 19, 29, 37, 43, 50, 58, 59, 61, 67, 75, and 98 bear evidence of Merton's competence and control in the use of the medium. Ansel Adams defines a great photograph as "a full expression of what one feels about what is being photographed in the deepest sense, and is thereby a true expression of what one feels about life in its entirety."[3]

Merton's photographs, especially his portraits, reveal not only his acute perception of the moment and feeling, but, more importantly, the particular quality of sensitivity in framing the essence of people and the environment. No intrusiveness or aggressiveness in his pictures, they disclose a sense of respect and ability to unfold something of the place, person, and object. His photography celebrates his awareness of "the wholeness of his communion with nature and with life."[4]

Thomas Merton's ascetic and poetic personality strips his photographs of redundancies, emotionalism, and triteness to invest them with mystery, innocence, and vision. His imagery generates a powerful sense of what he calls "infused contemplation,"[5] and a sense of "significant enigmas."[6] In addition to their technical mastery and formal beauty, images such as 4, 14, 16, 17, 32, 34, 37, 38, 56, 71, 73, or 98 convey "unique and unconscious harmonies appropriate to their own moment," though not confined to them, and awake "possibilities, consonances,"[7]—perhaps what Stieglitz meant when he talked about "equivalents." And, like this master of modern photography, Merton believed that all art is rooted in love, and as Ben Shahn testified, "a product of the spirit."[8] Father Louis's people, nature scenes, man-made objects, and abstract forms and designs manifest a feeling of sacredness, wonder, strength, and joy. They correlate the human drama with the cosmic drama. Invincibly centered in his eremitic life, Thomas Merton is yet able to achieve the "happiest consummation" as an artist in integrating his art "into an organic spiritual whole," and transforming it into " the most vital expression of a life of praise and worship."[9]

Deba P. Patnaik

Notes

Introduction

Italicized lines are from various poems of Thomas Merton

1. Thomas Merton, *The Monastic Journey,* edited by Brother Patrick Hart (Kansas City: Sheed Andrews & McMeel, Inc., 1977), p. 17.
2. Thomas Merton, *Conjectures of a Guilty Bystander* (New York: Doubleday Image Books, 1968), p. 308.
3. *Conjectures of a Guilty Bystander,* p. 307.
4. Edward Weston, "Seeing Photographically," *The Complete Photographer,* Vol. 9, No. 49, pp. 3200-3206.
5. Thomas Merton, *The Asian Journal* (New York: New Directions, 1968), p. 153.
6. *The Asian Journal,* pp. 156-57.
7. Thomas Merton, *Notes on Art and Worship* (mimeographed; Abbey of Gethsemani), p. 4.
8. *Notes on Art and Worship,* p. 21.
9. *Ibid,* p. 3.
10. Thomas Merton, *The Sign of Jonas* (New York: Harcourt, Brace & Co., 1953), p. 238.
11. *Notes on Art and Worship,* p. 36.
12. *Conjectures of a Guilty Bystander,* p. 7.
13. *The Sign of Jonas,* p. 238.
14. *Conjectures of a Guilty Bystander,* p. 221.
15. Thomas Merton, *New Seeds of Contemplation* (New York: New Directions, 1972), p. 23.
16. *Notes on Art and Worship,* pp. 1-2.
17. Thomas Merton, *Hagia Sophia* (Lexington, Kentucky: Stamperia del Santuccio, 1962), p. 1.
18. Thomas Merton, "Poetry and Contemplation: A Reappraisal," *Commonweal 69* (October 24, 1958), pp. 87-92.
19. Alfred Stieglitz, *Aperture,* 8:1, 1960, p. 36.
20. *The Sign of Jonas,* p. 233.
21. Thomas Merton, "Theology of Creativity," *The American Benedictine Review,* xi, 1960), pp. 197-213.
22. *Notes on Art and Worship,* p. 2.
23. *Ibid,* p. 2.
24. *The Sign of Jonas,* p. 48.
25. *Ibid,* p. 40.

Text

1. *New Seeds of Contemplation,* p. 297.
2. *The Asian Journal,* pp. 233-34.
3. Thomas Merton, *The Geography of Lograire* (New York: New Directions, 1969), pp. 41-42.
4. *The Sign of Jonas,* p. 361.
5. Thomas Merton, *Emblems of a Season of Fury* (New York: New Directions, 1963), p. 35.
6. Thomas Merton, "O Sweet Irrational Worship," *Collected Poems* (New York: New Directions, 1977), p. 34.
7. *The Asian Journal,* pp. 153-54.
8. Thomas Merton, *Love and Living* (New York: Farrar, Straus & Giroux, 1979), p. 120.
9. Thomas Merton, *The Strange Islands* (New York: New Directions, 1956), p. 42.
10. *New Seeds of Contemplation,* pp. 291-92.
11. Thomas Merton, *Raids on the Unspeakable* (New York: New Directions, 1966), pp. 106-07.
12. "The Night of Destiny," *Collected Poems,* p. 635.

Afterword

1. *Letters* to John Howard Griffin.
2. *Letters.* Also, in Griffin's *A Hidden Wholeness: The Visual World of Thomas Merton* (Boston: Houghton Mifflin Co., 1970), p. 3.
3. Ansel Adams, "A Personal Credo," *American Annual of Photography,* Vol. 58, pp. 7-16.
4. *Conjectures of a Guilty Bystander,* p. 307.
5. Thomas Merton, *What Is Contemplation?* (Notre Dame: St. Mary's Press, 1948).
6. *Conjectures of a Guilty Bystander,* p. 301.
7. *Raids on the Unspeakable,* pp. 181-2.
8. Ben Shahn, *Paragraphs on Art* (New York: Spiral Press, 1952), p. 1.
9. *The Sign of Jonas,* p. 49.

Photographs

1. California (Whitehorn)	1968
2. Polonnaruwa, Sri Lanka (Reclining Buddha and Standing Ananda)	1968
3. New Mexico	1968
4. New Delhi, India (*Jantar Mantar**)	1968
5. Gethsemani, Kentucky	1967
6. Gethsemani	1965
7. Gethsemani (Hermitage†)	1966
8. Gethsemani	1966
9. Darjeeling, India	1968
10. Darjeeling (Karlu Rimpoche)	1968
11. New Mexico	1968
12. Gethsemani (Old Sheep Barn)	1965
13. Gethsemani (Hermitage)	1966
14. Gethsemani (Old Novitiate House)	1965
15. Gethsemani (Hermitage)	1967
16. New Delhi *(Jantar Mantar)*	1968
17. Darjeeling	1968
18. Gethsemani	1964
19. Gethsemani	1964
20. Bardstown, Kentucky (Distillery)	1966
21. Bangkok, Thailand (The Temple of the Emerald Buddha)	1968
22. California or New Mexico	1968
23. Gethsemani	1966
24. Darjeeling (Khamtul Rimpoche)	1968
25. Darjeeling	1968
26. Polonnaruwa, Sri Lanka	1968
27. Polonnaruwa, Sri Lanka	1968
28. Darjeeling (the *Kanchenjunga*‡)	1968

*Jantar Mantar: observatory built approximately 1725 A.D. by Maharaja Jai Singh II of Jaipur.
† Hermitage: situated inside the Abbey of Gethsemani compound; Merton spent his last years there as a hermit.
‡ *Kanchenjunga:* 28,146 foot peak of the Himalayan mountain range, north of Darjeeling.

29.	Darjeeling (Terraced Plantation)	1968
30.	Bangkok	1968
31.	California	1968
32.	California	1968
33.	Gethsemani (Shops Building)	1965
34.	Shakertown, Kentucky	1965
35.	Gethsemani	1966
36.	Gethsemani (Hermitage)	1966
37.	Gethsemani (Hermitage)	1966
38.	New Mexico	1968
39.	Gethsemani (Tool Shed)	1967
40.	Alaska	1968
41.	New Mexico (Georgia O'Keeffe's House)	1968
42.	New Mexico	1968
43.	Darjeeling	1968
44.	Bardstown (Distillery)	1965
45.	Bardstown	1968
46.	Gethsemani	1966
47.	California (Redwoods)	1968
48.	Gethsemani	1964
49.	Gethsemani (Zen Garden)	1967
50.	Gethsemani (Zen Garden)	1967
51.	Gethsemani	1964
52.	India	1968
53.	Gethsemani	1966
54.	Gethsemani	1967
55.	Gethsemani	1965
56.	New Delhi (*Jantar Mantar*)	1968
57.	California	1968
58.	Darjeeling	1968
59.	New Mexico (*Christ in the Desert Monastery*)	1968
60.	New Mexico (*Christ in the Desert Monastery*)	1968
61.	Shakertown	1965
62.	Darjeeling	1968
63.	Darjeeling (10-year old *tulku**)	1968
64.	California	1968
65.	Gethsemani (Old Sheep Barn)	1965
66.	Gethsemani	1965
67.	Gethsemani	1965
68.	Gethsemani	1964
69.	California	1968
70.	California	1968
71.	California	1968
72.	Gethsemani	1963
73.	Calcutta, India	1968
74.	Gethsemani	1964

**Tulku:* A Tibetan word meaning "living Buddha;" it refers to the reincarnated soul of someone who had become very enlightened during an earlier incarnation.

75. Gethsemani (Railroad Station)	1965
76. Gethsemani	1967
77. Gethsemani	1964
78. India	1968
79. Jacques Maritain at Gethsemani	1966
80. Polonnaruwa	1968
81. Alaska	1968
82. Bangkok	1968
83. California	1968
84. Gethsemani	1965
85. Shakertown	1965
86. Gethsemani	1965
87. Darjeeling (Ratod Rimpoche)	1968
88. Darjeeling (Tibetan Prayer Flag Pole)	1968
89. Sri Lanka (Nyanaponika Thera with young *bhikku**)	1968
90. New Mexico	1968
91. Gethsemani (from Hermitage Porch)	1967
92. New Mexico	1968
93. California (Redwoods)	1968
94. Gethsemani	1963
95. New Mexico	1968
96. Gethsemani (Monastery Church)	1967
97. California	1968
98. California (Redwoods)	1968
99. California	1968
100. Gethsemani	1965

Bhikku: a Buddhist mendicant, monk.

Chronology

1915   January 31, birth in Prades, France; son of artist Ruth Jenkins of Zanesville, Ohio and artist Owen Merton of Christ Church, New Zealand.

1916   Baptism in Prades. Dr. T. Bennett of Harley Street, London is godfather. Moves to New York to live with mother's family in Douglaston, Long Island.

1918   Brother John Paul born.

1921   Mother's death.

1922   Attends elementary school in Bermuda.

1926   Enters Lycee Ingres, Montauban, France.

1929   Enters Oakham School, Rutland, England.

1931   Father's death. Stays with Dr. Bennett in London.

1932   Graduates from Oakham; scholarship to Clare College, Cambridge University.

1933   Trip to Italy and U. S. A. Enters Cambridge in the fall to study French and Italian in preparation for British Diplomatic Service, at Dr. Bennett's insistence.

1934   Gains second in Modern Language Tripos, Part I, at Cambridge. Moves back to New York.

1935   Enters Columbia University in February and meets Professor Mark Van Doren.

1936   Grandfather's death. Meets Robert Lax, Robert Giroux, Ed Rice, and Sy Freedgood.

1937   Grandmother's death. Editor of 1937 *Yearbook* and art editor of *Jester* at Columbia University. Meets Raissa Maritain. Becomes interested in Oriental religions, philosophy, and the spiritual life.

1938   Meets Brahmachari. Graduates from Columbia and begins work on M. A. in English. First Sunday Mass at the

Church of Corpus Christi, New York. Consults Fr. Ford to become a Catholic. Meets Dan Walsh, professor of philosophy at Columbia. November 16, baptism and First Communion at Corpus Christi with Ed Rice as godfather, and Lax and Freedgood present. Reviews books for *New York Times* and *New York Herald Tribune* until 1940.

1939   M.A. from Columbia. Teaches English in University Extension and at St. Bonaventure University until 1941.

1940   Meets Catherine de Hueck (Doherty); works at her Friendship House in Harlem, New York.

1941   Easter, first retreat at Gethsemani at the suggestion of Dan Walsh; decides to join as a monk. December 10, enters the Abbey of Gethsemani.

1943   April 17, John Paul's death.

1944   March 19, Simple Vows of Cistercian Order.
Thirty Poems, New Directions; poems.

1946   *A Man in the Divided Sea*, New Directions; second volume of poems.

1947   March 19, Solemn Vows.

1948   *Figures of an Apocalypse*, New Directions; poems.
The Seven Storey Mountain, Harcourt Brace Jovanovich; autobiography.
Exile Ends in Glory, Bruce; biography.

1949   May 26, ordained priest at Gethsemani with Van Doren, Lax, Rice, and Freedgood present. Golden Book Award by the Catholic Writers Guild of America for *The Seven Storey Mountain*.
Seeds of Contemplation, New Directions; religion.
The Waters of Siloe, Harcourt Brace Jovanovich; history.
The Tears of the Blind Lions, New Directions; poems.

1950   *What Are These Wounds?*, Bruce; biography.

1951   June 22, American citizenship in Louisville, Kentucky. Master of the Students, Gethsemani, until 1955. St. Francis de Sales Award by the Catholic Writers Guild of America for *The Ascent to Truth*.
The Ascent to Truth, Harcourt Brace Jovanovich; theology.

1953   *The Sign of Jonas*, Harcourt Brace Jovanovich; journal.
Bread in the Wilderness, New Directions; theology.

1954   Meets Victor Hammer.
The Last of the Fathers, Harcourt Brace Jovanovich; theology.

1955	Master of the Novices until 1965. *No Man Is an Island*, Harcourt Brace Jovanovich; religion.
1956	*The Living Bread*, Farrar, Straus & Giroux; theology. *The Strange Islands*, New Directions; poems.
1957	Meets Ernesto Cardenal as a postulant at Gethsemani. Goes to St. John's Abbey, Collegeville, Minnesota, and meets Dr. Gregory Zilboorg. *The Tower of Babel*, New Directions; poems. *The Silent Life*, Farrar, Straus & Giroux; religion.
1958	*Thoughts in Solitude*, Farrar, Straus & Giroux; religion.
1959	*The Secular Journal of Thomas Merton*, Farrar, Straus & Giroux; journal. *Selected Poems*, New Directions; poems.
1960	*Spiritual Direction and Meditation*, Liturgical Press; religion. *The Wisdom of the Desert*, New Directions; religion. *Disputed Questions*, Farrar, Straus & Giroux; essays.
1961	Meets John Howard Griffin after years of friendly correspondence. Awarded Medal for Excellence, Columbia University. Begins photographing, using Griffin's camera. *The Behavior of Titans*, New Directions; prose poems and essays. *New Seeds of Contemplation*, New Directions; religion. *The New Man*, Farrar, Straus & Giroux; religion.
1962	Meets Dan Berrigan. *Original Child Bomb*, New Directions; prose poem.
1963	*Life and Holiness*, Herder & Herder; religion. *Emblems of a Season of Fury*, New Directions, poems. *Breakthrough to Peace*, New Directions; edited.
1964	Meets Dr. D. Suzuki in New York. Honorary L. D., University of Kentucky. *Seeds of Destruction*, Farrar, Straus & Giroux; essays.
1965	August 20, retires to hermitage. *The Way of Chuan-Tzu*, New Directions; philosophy. *Seasons of Celebration*, Farrar, Straus & Giroux; religion.
1966	Meets Jacques Maritain after years of intimate correspondence. Meets Joan Baez, Sufi Master C. D. Abdesalam, and Vietnamese Buddhist monk Thich Nhat Hanh. *Raids on the Unspeakable*, New Directions; prose poems. *Conjectures of a Guilty Bystander*, Doubleday & Company; notes.

1967　　May, concelebrates Dan Walsh's ordination; preaches homily.
Mystics and Zen Masters, Farrar, Straus & Giroux; essays.

1968　　Trip to Christ in the Desert Monastery, New Mexico, Our Lady of the Redwoods Abbey, California, and Alaska. Starts a spiritual workshop for nuns at Yakutat, Alaska. First trip abroad as a Trappist. Travels to India, Japan, Sri Lanka, and Thailand. Addresses Spiritual Summit Conference of World Religions, Calcutta, India, and of Asian Benedictine and Cistercian nuns, monks, abbots in Bangkok, Thailand. Meets Dalai Lama, India.
Cables to the Ace, New Directions; prose poems.
Faith and Violence, University of Notre Dame Press; essays.
Zen and the Birds of Appetite, New Directions; essays.
December 10, death in Bangkok. December 17, burial at the Abbey of Gethsemani, Trappist, Kentucky.

PRODUCTION NOTES

The text type, 11 on 13 Helvetica Light, was set on the Linotron 606 by The Parthenon Press.
Halftones are 150 line screen; text stock is 80 lb. Karma Natural.
Printing and binding by the Halliday Lithograph Company.

Text design by T. Darwish.

Jacket design by the Joseph del Gaudio Design Group, Inc.